THE COCKS OF NAPTON LOCKS

THE COCKS OF NAPTON LOCKS

Michael Caton

Copyright © 2022 Michael Caton

The moral right of the author has been asserted.

Apart from any fair dealing for the purposes of research or private study, or criticism or review, as permitted under the Copyright, Designs and Patents Act 1988, this publication may only be reproduced, stored or transmitted, in any form or by any means, with the prior permission in writing of the publishers, or in the case of reprographic reproduction in accordance with the terms of licences issued by the Copyright Licensing Agency. Enquiries concerning reproduction outside those terms should be sent to the publishers.

Matador
Unit E2 Airfield Business Park,
Harrison Road, Market Harborough,
Leicestershire. LE16 7UL
Tel: 0116 2792299
Email: books@troubador.co.uk
Web: www.troubador.co.uk/matador
Twitter: @matadorbooks

ISBN 978 1803135 991

British Library Cataloguing in Publication Data.
A catalogue record for this book is available from the British Library.

Typeset in 11pt Minion Pro by Troubador Publishing Ltd, Leicester, UK

Matador is an imprint of Troubador Publishing Ltd

In memory of my much loved wife Margaret
1935-2022

About the author

A former vice-chairman of the National Council on Inland Transport, Michael Caton has been a longstanding advocate for canal and rail transport. Combining this with his interest in history and family ancestry, The Cocks of Napton Locks represents many years of meticulous research.

Map of Oxford Canal by Location Maps Ltd

Introduction

The village of Napton on the Hill on the Oxford Canal in South Warwickshire is a delightful place well known to narrowboat enthusiasts. At Napton the canal passes through seven locks and three generations of my family were lock carpenters there spanning the years 1833 to 1938. Some memories of those years have been handed down to me through the family and linking these together with available records, including those from the canal company and census returns, has produced an interesting story with insights into life and canal history of the period.

The original family name of the three lock carpenters, Thomas, Joseph and Sidney, was Cock and Marian, daughter of Joseph, was my maternal grandmother. I should explain that about 1881 the name was changed to Cocks, the 's' being added to please Annie, wife of Joseph.

The book includes photographs dating from 1886 to the present day. Some of the historical photographs were taken by family members with a box camera and hence their quality does not match modern images. Others are reproductions of old postcards. The recent photographs were taken by my son Peter.

The Locks, Napton, 1938. From an old postcard.

The Locks, Napton, 2022.

The Locks, Napton, 1996 (Photo Paul Cocks).

The Cocks Family Tree

The family tree on the following page shows the relationships of the various family members referred to in the text. Other sons of the family also worked as carpenters, probably as apprentices learning the job from their father. Those family members known to have worked in this capacity are indicated on the family tree.

Birth dates are given where these are available otherwise baptism dates are given. As baptisms usually took place a short time after the birth they probably were in the same year except perhaps near the year end when they could have been held over to the next year. Those dates that refer to baptisms are marked with the letter 'b'.

COCK(S) FAMILY TREE

*Thomas Cock
1796-1866
=Sarah Copson
1801-1892

- Thomas 1824b- =Mary Garrett 1841-1904
- Catherine 1826b-1921 =Richard Reynolds
- Esther 1828b-1869 =William Juggins
- John 1831b-1847
- Mary 1835-1833?
- William 1836b-
- Jane 1838-1849
- *Joseph 1841-1911 =Annie Garrett

Children of Thomas & Mary Garrett:
- Victor

Children of Joseph & Annie Garrett:
- *Copson 1866-1893
- *Sidney 1869-1940
- Marian 1872-1964 =Edward Burnham

Children of Sidney:
- Marjorie 1903-1994 =Cyril Caton 1904-1947
- Phyllis 1908-2000 =Leonard Taylor
- Harold 1910-1980

Francis

Elsie

Eric =Lily Burnett -1935

Dorothy =Clem Thomas

Michael 1935-

Margaret 1938-1997

Rita 1941-2014

Cyril =Ruth

Paul 1935-2005

Mary 1935-

After Cyril Caton & Lily Cocks died, Eric Cocks & Marjorie Caton married each other.

Other children descended from Sidney Cocks:
Philip – son of Cyril & Ruth
Eunice – daughter of Elsie
Christine – daughter of Dorothy & Clem

b Baptism date
*Worked as carpenter at Napton

History of the Oxford Canal

One of the earliest cuts of the canal age, the building of the Oxford Canal Navigation, as it was originally known, was approved by Act of Parliament in 1769. Work commenced in 1770 and the ninety one mile route opened in sections from 1774, finally linking Oxford and Coventry on 1st January 1790. The original engineer was James Brindley who received a salary of £200 per year. After he died suddenly in 1772 at the age of fifty six, his brother-in-law Samuel Simcock took over.

The canal followed a circuitous route along the 300ft contour line from Longford in Coventry as far as Hillmorton Locks and it was said that a boatman could travel for a whole day within the sound of the bells of the church of St John the Baptist in the village of Brinklow between Coventry and Rugby. The explanation for this tortuous line is unclear, as when building earlier canals Brindley had not adhered so tightly to contours but he may have had to choose such a route for economy as cuttings and embankments are costly to build and maintain. The choice of route however meant that the canal missed passing through many villages and the long transit times were unpopular. In the 1830s William Cubitt and Marc Brunel were therefore engaged to straighten parts of Brindley's original line, making use of new developments in engineering.

Also in the 1830s, the stretch between Napton and Braunston, where the canal shares its route with the busy Grand Union Canal, was widened. The southern section between Napton and Oxford however remains remarkably unspoilt and offers an evocative insight into 19th century canal life.

Providing a direct link with London via the Thames, the Oxford Canal was initially hugely profitable and showed a profit even before completion. The arrival of the Grand Junction Canal (later renamed Grand Union) effectively bypassed the southern half of the Oxford Canal, taking traffic and breaking its stranglehold. The Grand Union also had the advantage of joining the Thames further downstream, so missing the less easily navigated section south of Oxford.

Trade began to seriously decline after World War II and commercial transport of goods by canal fell dramatically throughout the 1960s, with last carrying companies struggling on until 1970. The future for canals looked bleak but the British Waterways Board, founded in 1965, had been tasked with developing and maintaining certain canals, including the Oxford, for leisure purposes and slowly the numbers of people using the waterways for pleasure boating began to rise. The Oxford Canal is now a popular route for narrowboat holidays.

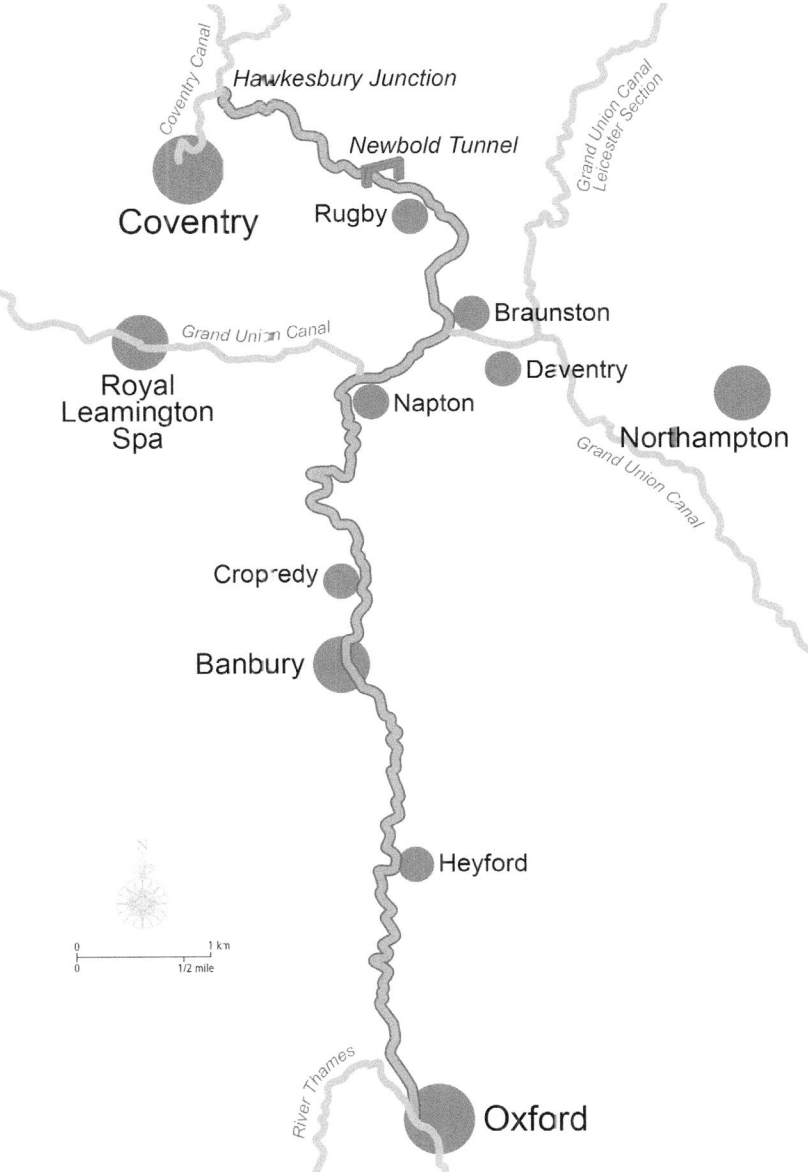

A Brief History of Napton

More properly known as Napton-on-the-Hill, the village was recorded in the Domesday Book as Neptone. Archaeological finds date back to Neolithic and Bronze Age times and it is probable that an Iron Age fort once stood on the hill.

Unusually the current population of around a thousand is similar to that recorded in the Middle Ages, when it was one of the largest towns in Warwickshire. Two buildings dominate the village, the Church of St Lawrence and the windmill.

The church dates back to the twelfth century, although was rebuilt in the following century and various additions have been made since. There are six bells in the tower, four of which were cast by Thomas Russell in 1731. According to legend it was intended for the church to be built close to the current village green but three times the stones were laid out ready and three times the fairies moved them overnight to the top of the hill. Not wanting to battle the spirits it was constructed on the hill, commanding a fine view in all directions.

Records show that a windmill has stood on the hill since at least 1543, although the current structure is more recent. It was operated by sail until 1900, then by steam for a further nine years. After falling into disrepair it was renovated as a dwelling, for which it is still used today.

During World War Two an observation post was set up on the hill near the windmill and although this is on private land visitors are permitted to use a seat here and to enjoy the view.

Beside the canal below the windmill was a brickworks, which once employed 110 people and had its own wharf. It closed in 1973.

Encircling the village on three sides, the Oxford Canal has been an important part of Napton's history since 1774, bringing trade, employment and more latterly pleasure cruisers.

Napton Windmill, 2022.

The Thomas Cock Period

1833 – 1865

The story begins with Thomas Cock who was born at Hillmorton near Rugby in 1796. His parents were John and Elizabeth Cock, John being employed as a labourer. The Cock family lived in Hillmorton for many years where there were Cocks at least as far back as the early years of the eighteenth century. Thomas and his family moved to Napton, probably in 1833, to take up the job of lock carpenter there. Nothing of Thomas' earlier career is known but as Hillmorton, like Napton, is on the Oxford Canal and has three locks, it is likely that he learned the skills of the trade and undertook carpentry work there.

I established the probable year of the move to Napton in a conversation with my second cousin, Elsie, Sidney's daughter. She told me that Catherine, the eldest daughter of Thomas, who was baptised in 1826 and whom she knew as Aunt Kate, had said to her that she was seven years old when they came to live at the Locks Napton. Records in the Napton parish registers show that Catherine's younger sister Mary was baptised on 26th August 1833 at Napton, so presumably the move took place before that date.

My mother, Marjorie, also remembered Aunt Kate who, she told me, had an old fashioned ear trumpet and gave her sweets with soft centres. In her later years Aunt Kate lived at nearby Southam. She died in 1921 at the advanced age of ninety five, having lived from Regency times and the era of the stage coach to the advent of the aeroplane and the wireless.

The lock carpenters and their families lived in a house called the Locks by the bottom lock at Napton. This still stands and is now a private residence. At the time of the Cocks family it was two houses, the other being occupied by the lock keepers. There is a bridge nearby crossed by a road from the village to a pub which was then called the Bull and Butcher and is now The Folly.

At the time of the move Thomas and his wife Sarah, who he married at Hillmorton Church in 1820, had four children; Thomas, Catherine, Esther and John. They later had four more; Mary, William, Jane and Joseph who was my great grandfather. The 1841 census records show that all eight children were then living with their parents at the Locks and the eldest, Thomas is recorded as working as a carpenter.

Joseph, the youngest child was born in 1841. There is an interesting record of his birth in the form of a piece of embroidery stitched by Aunt Kate of which a photo is shown below. This was handed down through the family and is now in my possession. It was given to me by my Auntie Phyllis, younger daughter of Marian, who told me that Aunt Kate embroidered it at the age of 18. That would have been in 1844 when Joseph was 3 years old. However there is a bit of a mystery here since, as explained above, the 's' was not added to the name until the 1880s.

By the time of the 1851 census only four children were resident at the Locks: Mary, William, Joseph and Catherine who by then had married

Embroidery by Catherine Reynolds (Aunt Kate).

silk merchant Richard Reynolds and had a one month old baby Francis. Thomas junior had moved away from home as had Esther who was married in 1849 and John and Jane had died.

It is interesting to note that at the time of the 1851 census a boat legger, Thomas Wickson and a Primitive Methodist itinerant preacher Henry Yeates were staying with the family.

It is worth pausing to ponder what would have been busy scene at Napton at the time Thomas and family arrived there. The Oxford Canal had only been open throughout its whole length for forty three years and canal transport was in its heyday, providing the transport arteries of Britain in the early years of the Industrial Revolution. Railway competition had hardly started, the first railway from Stockton to Darlington having opened only eight years earlier and the main line from London to Birmingham was not to open for another five years. The latter railway passes close to the canal at Hillmorton and Thomas and family no doubt saw it under construction when they were living there.

No memories of Thomas have survived through the family, however there are references to work undertaken by him in the 1865-1870 day book of the Oxford Canal. The day books record details of payments for work undertaken on the canal and are a very useful source of information. There are several entries of payments to Thomas in 1865, the last of these being on 25th July of that year, when he presumably retired, since the first payment to Joseph was on 2nd September.

Thomas and his son William are named in a list of Oxford Canal employees for the year 1853. As far as is known, this is one of only two years for which lists exist, the other being 1924. Thomas' son John was a carpenter at the time of his early death in 1847 aged 17.

Some of the tools used on the locks are still held by the family including a trysquare on the handle of which is inscribed the name 'Thomas Cock'.

Thomas died in 1866 aged 69.

The Folly (formerly the Bull and Butcher), 2022.

The Locks Cottage

The original cottage is thought to pre-date the canal, with the second added so that both the lock keeper and carpenters, plus their families, could be accommodated. Whilst there is no obvious indication from outside that the house was once two separate cottages, inside several steps down to the kitchen indicate that they were on different levels.

A vaulted-roofed cellar under the cottage may have been a workshop for the carpenters. The building on the opposite bank is however currently employed as a workshop, so may have been used by the lock carpenters, although it has been suggested that a window high on the south wall might indicate that this floor was once lived in.

The single storey pitch roofed room on the south side of the Locks was once a laundry. The tall chimney behind this has now gone but other than this the exterior of house appears remarkably similar to when the Cocks families lived here. Whilst the large tree in the garden has gone, it is noticeable in recent photographs that many trees have grown up along the canal and hillside.

Adjacent to the cottage was a pumping system used to replace water in the canal lost by operation of the locks. This is still in place but has been superseded by a more modern system.

When I visited in 1996 the cottage had been painted white and contained a small shop.

The grade II listed house was purchased by Nigel Wood in 2007, at which time it was semi-derelict. He has extensively renovated the building and it is now a fine residence, which he calls Napton Lock Cottage. The stables at the rear, which once housed horses working on the canal, have been converted into accommodation for two people and is let for holidays, proving to be very popular.

A Link with Thomas Guy

Thomas Guy, founder of Guy's Hospital in London was Member of Parliament for Tamworth in Staffordshire and a great benefactor to that town. He built some almshouses there, erection of which commenced in 1673. Initially there were houses to accommodate seven poor women, residences for men being added in 1692. Guy was elected as the town's MP six times but when the local electors changed their voting habits at the 1708 election he was defeated. He was appalled at this after all he had done for the town and when he died in 1724 left directions excluding the people of Tamworth from the almshouses, which were only to be for his own relations and for 'hamleteers' i.e. people from the surrounding villages of Wilnecote, Glascote, Bolehall, Amington, Wiggington and Hopwas.

My mother told me that the eldest member of our family is eligible to live in the Thomas Guy almshouses. As she was the eldest member of her generation (children of Marian and Edward) she thought the privilege applied to her. This information had clearly been handed to her from her own mother, Marian. However it was difficult to see how the family living at Napton some thirty miles away would qualify for Thomas Guy's admission rules.

I decided to delve into this and the clue came from investigating what became of Sarah Cock after Thomas' death in 1866. I was unable to find any reference to her in the census returns for the Napton area but on browsing through the Oxford Canal day books I came across many references to payment of her pension. The first of these was on December 29th 1866 and they continued until 1892 when she died aged 92. The pension payments were usually made at four or five weekly intervals at the rate of six shillings a week.

However the day books give no indication of where Sarah was living. I then searched the census returns and to my surprise found that in the 1871 and 1891 censuses she was resident at the Tamworth Alms Houses.

I then needed to find out how she had the right to live there since, as far as I am aware, Napton had no connection with Thomas Guy. This became apparent when I discovered that her mother, Sarah Copson, 1776-1856, had also been resident there, as recorded in the 1851 census. Sarah Copson had also lived at Napton, prior to moving to the almshouses, but she was born at Wilncote near Tamworth, one of the villages on Thomas Guy's permitted list. Her maiden name was Middleton and she married John Copson at Tamworth in 1791, moving to Napton sometime in the next ten years, as is clear from the fact that their daughter was born there in 1799.

It is interesting to speculate why the couple made what would have been quite a major move at that time. John was a blacksmith and it is possible that he was employed in that capacity by the canal company in the very early days of the Oxford Canal. If that was the case it would be another very interesting link with the family and the canal in a role complementing that of the lock carpenters.

The Tamworth almshouses continued in use until 1913 when they were demolished and new ones built on the same site. I have visited these and was welcomed and able to explain the connection with our family.

The Joseph Cocks Years

1865-1911

As mentioned, it is clear from the Oxford Canal Day Book that Joseph succeeded his father Thomas as lock carpenter in 1865 and he held this position until his own death in 1911.

Many memories of Joseph have been passed down through the family. My mother, Marjorie, who knew him as Grandpa Cocks, remembered him well although she was only seven years old when he died. She often used to talk about him and said that he was tall and had a beard. She told me he used to say 'well well well'! She recalled visiting Napton from her home in Birmingham and having strawberries and cream for tea, with strawberries from Grandpa's garden.

Joseph married Annie Garrett and they had three children: Copson, Sidney and Marian. It is interesting that Joseph's elder brother Thomas married Annie Garrett's younger sister Mary. The wedding was in 1873, relatively late in life for Thomas who was then aged forty nine. The couple emigrated to Australia. They had a son Victor who Elsie told me was in the forces during the First World War when he came to England and visited the family.

Joseph, Anne and their children are recorded as living at the Locks in the 1871 and 1881 censuses, but in 1891 they were on their own, the children having left home by then. In 1871 and 1881 an aunt of Annie, Ann Pinder who was a shoemaker's widow, was living with them. Investigations of the 1851 census returns showed that her husband John was a cordwainer (shoemaker) at Ilkeston in Derbyshire.

Marian, my grandmother, who spent her adult life in the Birmingham area, had very fond memories of her childhood days at Napton and often used to talk about them right into her old age. Joseph and Annie's two boys Copson and Sidney were educated at the village school but Marian was sent away to Old Arnold High School in Rugby where she was a weekly boarder. It is not known why they decided to give the girl a private education; rather the opposite of what might have been expected within the social structure of the period. It is evident to me that her schooling gave her lifelong interests she probably wouldn't have otherwise had; I remember her interest in history and I have her copy of The Poetical Works of Henry Wadsworth Longfellow published in 1889. She played the piano and I remember the family gathering round her to sing hymns and songs.

The two boys used to play tricks on Marian and one day, when she was crossing a plank bridge across a brook in her best clothes on her way to Sunday school, they shook the plank and she fell into the water. However they were quick to stand up for her when she was threatened by other boys.

The group family photo, taken outside the Locks cottage, (page 22) can be dated at 1886/7 thanks to my grandmother, born in 1872, who told my mother that she was aged fourteen when it was taken. She also said that the little boy in the centre of the picture happened to be with them at the time and was not a member of the family.

There is another photo on page 21 taken outside of the Locks with Joseph Cocks and his second wife Francis, which would have taken between 1904 and 1911.

Napton has a fine windmill on the hill above the village which in those days was operational. Marian had a friend there who she would go and stay with for weekends. Later the windmill fell into disuse but happily is now restored as a residence.

Much information on the work of Joseph is recorded in the canal archives. Commencing in 1865 there are numerous records in the Oxford Canal Day Books of payments to him for jobs undertaken. The work timetable for June 1904 (below), kept at the County Record Office Warwick, gives the location of his activities on each day of that month with some indication of the materials used.

TIME TABLE kept by L. Cocks

June 1904

Day of Month	Where working.	Labourers.	Material used.
1	Shop		One swing bail for Stable
2	Second Lock		Oak 5½ x 6½ 6-0, two gao spikes
3	9ⁿ lock	two	One Paddle start, one ½ plate 7 x 13
4	Shop		Six ⅝ x 3" woodscrews
5			
6	Do		
7	Third lock & G Eadons		Two line posts &c
8	Shop		One Paddle catch & bolt
9	8" lock N 3 Mile Ba one C		One plate for collar arms
10	Shop		
11	Do		
12			
13	Do		
14	9ⁿ lock		One large iron plate & spikes
15	Mr Tolleys House		Painting &c
16	Do		
17	Do		
18	Shop		
19			
20	Cabbage turn		
21	Do		
22	Do		
23	Shop		
24	M Doles		
25	4ⁿ lock		
26			
27	M Doles		
28	Do		
29	Do		
30	Do		
31			

The following letter from Joseph Cocks to R Gillett in 1883 regarding work on Broadmoor Lock, which is held at the British Waterways Archive, gives some idea of the carpenters' craft and the intricacies of lock construction and repair.

Napton 13th Nov 1883

Sir,

I find according to the plan of Broadmoor Top Gate its 6ft 2in from top of old sill to the proposed top of collar plate.

The top gate at our 7th lock is 5ft 9 from top of sill to top of collar plate so that the new sill will require to be 5 in deeper that is if it is put on the old sill.

If the new sill was cut the same size as the old one and raised by putting brickwork on the old head it would weaken the sill when struck by the boats because there would be no depth of sheeting at the back of it to support it. We have one done in this way and it always leaks.

The frost was very sharp last night the ice was quite strong and has not melted during the day. If it comes as sharp to night I expect the boatmen will want some assistance.

I am your obedient servant,
J. Cocks
To R. Gillett Esq.

The photo on page 22 showing Joseph and his colleagues working on one of the lock gates gives some insight into the lock carpenter's craft.

Joseph was, until 1899, a Congregationalist lay preacher in the Napton District. However he had been feeling uneasy at the beliefs of the Church when a pamphlet 'Christ in the earth again' by Robert Roberts of the Christadelphian community fell into his hands, as if by chance, at a friend's house while searching for another book. This reflected his own beliefs and way of thinking and led him to found the Christadelphian

The Locks, Napton, taken between 1904 & 1911. Joseph Cocks (left).

The Locks, Napton, 2022.

meeting in Napton which continues to worship in the Christadelphian Hall in the village, built on the site of the old smithy and opened in 1903, (photo below).

Joseph was described in the Christadelphian magazine of 1899 as '*a man of standing, distinguished by that beautiful blend of intelligence and devout disinterested 'zeal of God' alias 'good ground' from which the fruits of the spirit may be developed*'. His daughter Marian said how hard he studied and his achievements were remarkable for a man with only a basic education, living in a remote village with no doubt long and demanding hours spent on his job at the locks. He was a real stalwart of the Christadelphian community and proclaimed the faith as a speaker at internal meetings and public lectures.

Napton had a railway station on the Weedon Junction to Leamington line. However this was three miles away from the village and visitors arriving by train were met with a pony and trap. An interesting

The Christadelphian Hall, Napton. From an old postcard (date unknown).

The Christadelphian Hall, Napton, 2022.

observation in the Christadelphian Magazine of 1903 states that the *'evening meeting (at Napton) to commence about 5.30 and close at 7 O'clock, which will give ample time for anyone wishing to walk to Napton Station to meet the 8.13 train for Leamington, which reaches Birmingham at 10 O'clock'.*

There is a letter, held in our family for many years, from Brother Ladson of the Christadelphian community to his sister Fan, dated 24th May 1905 which gives a glimpse of the Napton scene of a hundred years ago. He had cycled from his home in Birmingham to speak at the Christadelphian meeting at Napton, and reported as follows:

> *'passing through Radford and Southam, I came into the country of canals, and saw the bold outline of the great windmill that I remembered on my last visit. A few more hilly miles and I reached Napton, and was welcomed by bro. Cocks and his pretty little housekeeper who has been ill and is still weak.*

The place is just the same, only that one of the cats is dead and the trees are all in leaf. It is one of the loveliest spots on earth, I feel sure. The may is out on the hedges, and the crab apples, also in the hedges. It looks lovely. The blossom is the same as ordinary apple bloom. I went to bed at ten, after a real cyclist's tea and supper. They are both most kind.

The scene from my window next morning was beyond words. The hills and the canal and the masses of green leaves and the red houses and the blue sky and sheep and cattle and birds, all made up a scene of loveliest, softest and most peaceful beauty. I just kneeled at the window and let the beauty work into my soul. Truly, it is a beautiful world.'

I should explain that Annie Cocks had died in 1904, the year before this letter was written. The name of the housekeeper referred to was Francis, who Joseph subsequently married. They are shown together in the photo below.

Joseph Cocks and second wife Francis. At the Locks, Napton, sometime between 1904 and 1911.

Joseph and Annie Cocks and children Sidney (left), Copson (back), Marian (right). Small boy in front was a visitor. At the Locks, Napton, 1886/7.

Working on the lock gate, Napton, Joseph Cocks, Lock Carpenter (right of centre). From an old postcard.

The Thomas Garit Chest

The oldest known link between the Cocks lock carpenters and the history of Napton, dating back to long before the building of the canal, is through the family of Joseph's wife Annie Garrett. Visitors to Napton Church will probably have noticed a large chest (photo page 25), on which is inscribed 'THOMAS GARIT OF NAPTON YEMAN AND ISABEL HIS WIFE GAVE THIS CHEST FOR THE VSE OF THIS CHVRCH IN TOKEN OF THEAR LOVES TO THIS PLASE 1624.' The oak chest is kept on the left of the chancel and is still used for storage by the church. It has two locks, one for which the vicar has a key and the other the churchwarden.

My mother told me that Thomas Garit was our ancestor, information she would have been handed down from her own mother. However there is no way of establishing how this entered the family memory. It seems unlikely that it was passed down from generation to generation over such a long period of time and it seems more probable that it was simply noted that the name was similar. The different spelling of the name is of no significance since this could easily have changed on transcription.

A search of the Napton parish registers revealed that Thomas and Isobel Garrett (here spelt as in our family) were living in Napton at that period and that Thomas was buried at Napton in 1648. The registers show that Garretts had been living in the area throughout the intervening period up until the time of Anne. Anne's parents were William and Charlotte Garrett and they lived in the High Street Napton. The 1861 census records that William was a sawer.

Napton Church. From an old postcard.

Napton Church, 2022.

Thomas Garit Chest, Napton Church. From an old postcard.

Thomas Garit Chest, Napton Church, Decorated for the Platinum Jubilee, June 2022.

The Sidney Cocks Years

1911–1938

Joseph Cocks' elder son Copson worked as an apprentice lock carpenter, as recorded in the 1881 census. He later moved to Birmingham, as recorded in the 1891 census and died of tuberculosis in 1893 at the age of twenty seven. My grandmother used to say that the illness had been made worse as a result of living by the canal. My mother used to talk about him as Uncle Copson, although she never met him, his death being ten years before she was born.

It was Joseph's younger son Sidney who succeeded his father as lock carpenter at Napton and he held the position until his retirement in 1938. Prior to moving to Napton he had worked as a carpenter in Birmingham; the photo on page 31 was taken during that period about 1900.

This is where my own memory comes in as I just remember seeing Uncle Sidney, shortly after his retirement, on a family visit to Napton. He died in 1940.

There are many entries in the Oxford Canal Day Book of work undertaken by Sidney, including the following recorded over the years 1929-1935. Unlike the nineteenth century day books at the time of Joseph, these give details of the work undertaken.

Extracts From Oxford Canal Day Book

- *June 3rd 1929 Repairs to Napton 6th Top Gate*
- *May 7th Reconstruction of Top Lock side with concrete blocks*
- *July 29th – August 3rd Napton Lock August 29th reconstruction of 7th Lock wall offside at Napton with concrete blocks*
- *April 22nd and 23rd 1930 Napton 4th lock putting in new fits to bottom gates*
- *June 10th – 11th 1930 7th Napton 7th lock splicing bottom gate head at stoppage*
- *April May and June 1930 repairing Napton 2nd Lock top gate 1 new oak head foot plank top bar and planking*
- *August 5th and 6th 1930 Marston Doles Lock putting in new bottom gate fits and filling*
- *August 1930 Repairs to Napton 4th Lock top gate and fixing*
- *September 1930 Renewing roof of Paint Shop Braunton September 1930*
- *October 1930 Repairs and decoration of Calcats lock house*
- *December 1930 Repairs to top gate 7th lock Napton December 1930 December 1930*
- *May 1931 Repairs to Napton 2nd lock bottom gate Whitsun stoppage*
- *August 1931 Putting new fits at bottom gates Napton 6th lock August*
- *April 1935 Napton 3rd lock Break down old lock side and rebuilding in concrete blocks*

My mother, who lived in Birmingham during her childhood, often mentioned the happy holidays she spent staying at the Locks during this period. She told me how they would enjoy playing hide and seek there. In the evenings the boat people passing through Napton would moor by the nearby bridge and entertain themselves with music from their concertina. She recalled an occasion during the First World War when they were driving along the road and met the authorities who took the horse off them for the war effort.

Outings in those days were a simple pleasure. The family took out a boat along the canal, accompanied by music from their gramophone. They had an organ which they placed on the ice boat and cruised along, hauled by their donkey, as they played and sang hymns.

Eunice Boff, daughter of Elsie and granddaughter of Sidney, lived at the Locks during her childhood in the 1930s and had many memories of that period. Two photos she took in 1937 show her grandfather at work. In the photo on page 30, in which he has the wage packets in his hand, he is with Wincelas Lines, known as 'Wink' Lines, the blacksmith who made all the metal work for the lock gates. The photo shows a lock gate under construction which was the last one Sidney made. There was a blacksmith's shop on the site at the Locks and Eunice recalled watching Mr Lines shaping pieces of iron for various items, as well as the lock gates. In the other photo on page 29 Sidney is with lengthman Harry Thornicroft, who was known as 'Harry Boy', and lived about the 6th lock.

Eunice also explained the various features of the photo on page x which shows the Locks in 1938, about the time of Sidney's retirement. The buildings on the left, close to the canal, have since been demolished. The large one of these, right by the canal, was the tar shed used for treating wood etc. The smaller one, set back from the canal, housed the hemp, the chalico (a mixture of tar and horse manure) and all the equipment for caulking the boats i.e. ramming hemp etc. into the joints between the planks on the side of the boat.

On the right, with a tall chimney was the kitchen for the right hand half of the cottage; they had to come out of the house to go to the kitchen.

The white railings were to stop the horses from falling into the bottom of the bank. The small window in the roof is where there was a small room. The low building on the right of the house was stables for the horses.

Sidney's elder son Cyril was, for a period, the lock keeper at Napton.

Sidney's retirement ended the one hundred and six year association of the Cocks lock carpenters with Napton. However the carpenter's craft continued in the family; Eric, Sidney's younger son had a career as a carpenter in the hotel trade in Torquay when he used tools used on the locks and Eric's grandson David continues to this day in the family tradition as a carpenter in Hereford.

Sidney Cocks, Lock Carpenter (left) and Harry Thornicroft, Lengthman (right), 1937 (Photo Eunice Boff).

Sidney Cocks, Lock Carpenter (left) and Wincelas Line, Blacksmith (right), 1937 (Photo Eunice Boff).

Sidney and Christiana Cocks and children Eric (left), Elsie (front), and Cyril (centre back). c1900.

Michael Caton (author)(right), Paul Cocks, his second wife Barbara (left), Mary McPherson (nee Cocks) and her husband Gordon. Napton, Sept. 1996 (Photo Margaret Caton).

Acknowledgements

I am indebted to the family members mentioned in the text for the information they gave to me which linked to the records, enabled this interesting story to be written.

I also wish to thank the many other people who helped me in various ways and in particular my son Peter (*www.petercatonbooks.co.uk*) for his assistance in getting the book published.

Also to the Canal River Trust (*www.canalrivertrust.org.uk*) and Rose Narrowboats (*www.rose.narrowboats.co.uk*) from whose websites information was obtained on the history of the Oxford Canal, and to Nigel Wood, current owner of 'The Locks' (*www.homeaway.co.uk – The Stables*).

For exclusive discounts on Matador titles,
sign up to our occasional newsletter at
troubador.co.uk/bookshop